Our Family Tree

ISBN 0-7858-1933-9   Library of Congress Card No. 77-78956

Manufactured in the United States of America

OUR FAMILY TREE

This Book is Lovingly Dedicated to:

_____

This record was compiled by:

_____

_____

and started on _____

A family record is more than names, dates and places. It is about people—what they did, the why and the how. This book is designed so you can record forever, in one volume, the history of your family and your ancestors.

There are sections where you can enter the origins of your family: where your ancestors came from and when, what happened to them, and the things they did. You will also be able to record, perhaps for the first time, stories about members of your family that have been handed down from preceding generations. There are other sections devoted to family photographs, traditions and such memorable events as weddings and reunions. And there is a most important "how to" section

that will help you trace your family's history: where to write and obtain records, what information to include in such inquiries, and what institutions are available to you for further assistance (such as libraries, and bookstores that specialize in genealogy information).

From the birth of a great, great grandparent to the birth of the newest baby in your family, this book provides a wonderful opportunity to gather together in one place all the interesting and unusual aspects of your family's history. When complete, it will be a storehouse of treasured information, achievements and memories—a permanent record of your family which is unique and not like any other.

CONTENTS

OUR FAMILY

This certifies that

_____

and

_____

Were United in Holy Matrimony

Place of Ceremony_____

City_____ State _____

Month_____Day_____Year_____

Married by _____

_____

HUSBAND'S GENEALOGY

Husband's Full Name _____

_____

Birth Date _____

Birth Place _____

Father's Full Name _____

Mother's Full Name _____

Brothers and Sisters _____

_____

_____

_____

WIFE'S GENEALOGY

Wife's Full Name _____

_____

Birth Date _____

Birth Place _____

Father's Full Name _____

Mother's Full Name _____

Brothers and Sisters _____

_____

_____

_____

OUR CHILDREN

Full Name	Place of Birth	Date of Birth

OUR GRANDCHILDREN & DESCENDANTS

_____

_____

_____

_____

_____

_____

_____

_____

_____

_____

_____

_____

_____

_____

_____

_____

OUR
FAMILY TREE

Husband's Full Name

Wife's Full Name

Date of Marriage   Place of Marriage

Our Children

WHO WE ARE
AND WHERE WE CAME FROM

Husband's Paternal Grandfather's Full Name

Husband's Paternal Grandmother's Full Name

Date of Marriage   Place of Marriage

Children

Husband's Father's Full Name

Husband's Mother's Full Name

Date of Marriage   Place of Marriage

Children

Husband's Maternal Grandfather's Full Name

Husband's Maternal Grandmother's Full Name

Date of Marriage   Place of Marriage

Children

THE PRECEDING 3 GENERATIONS ON THE FOLLOWING PAGE

Wife's Paternal Grandfather's Full Name

Wife's Paternal Grandmother's Full Name

Date of Marriage   Place of Marriage

Children

Wife's Father's Full Name

Wife's Mother's Full Name

Date of Marriage   Place of Marriage

Children

Wife's Maternal Grandfather's Full Name

Wife's Maternal Grandmother's Full Name

Date of Marriage   Place of Marriage

Children

Husband's Great Grandfather's Full Name

Husband's Great Grandmother's Full Name

Husband's Great Grandfather's Full Name

Husband's Great Grandmother's Full Name

Husband's Great Grandfather's Full Name

Husband's Great Grandmother's Full Name

Husband's Great Grandfather's Full Name

Husband's Great Grandmother's Full Name

Husband's Great, Great Grandfather's Full Name

Husband's Great, Great Grandmother's Full Name

Husband's Great, Great Grandfather's Full Name

Husband's Great, Great Grandmother's Full Name

Husband's Great, Great Grandfather's Full Name

Husband's Great, Great Grandmother's Full Name

Husband's Great, Great Grandfather's Full Name

Husband's Great, Great Grandmother's Full Name

Husband's Great, Great Grandfather's Full Name

Husband's Great, Great Grandmother's Full Name

Husband's Great, Great Grandfather's Full Name

Husband's Great, Great Grandmother's Full Name

Husband's Great, Great Grandfather's Full Name

Husband's Great, Great Grandmother's Full Name

Husband's Great, Great Grandfather's Full Name

Husband's Great, Great Grandmother's Full Name

Wife's Great Grandfather's Full Name

Wife's Great Grandmother's Full Name

Wife's Great Grandfather's Full Name

Wife's Great Grandmother's Full Name

Wife's Great Grandfather's Full Name

Wife's Great Grandmother's Full Name

Wife's Great Grandfather's Full Name

Wife's Great Grandmother's Full Name

Wife's Great, Great Grandfather's Full Name

Wife's Great, Great Grandmother's Full Name

Wife's Great, Great Grandfather's Full Name

Wife's Great, Great Grandmother's Full Name

Wife's Great, Great Grandfather's Full Name

Wife's Great, Great Grandmother's Full Name

Wife's Great, Great Grandfather's Full Name

Wife's Great, Great Grandmother's Full Name

Wife's Great, Great Grandfather's Full Name

Wife's Great, Great Grandmother's Full Name

Wife's Great, Great Grandfather's Full Name

Wife's Great, Great Grandmother's Full Name

Wife's Great, Great Grandfather's Full Name

Wife's Great, Great Grandmother's Full Name

Wife's Great, Great Grandfather's Full Name

Wife's Great, Great Grandmother's Full Name

Mr. & Mrs.	NEE
Mr. & Mrs.	NEE
Mr. & Mrs.	NEE
Mr. & Mrs.	NEE
Mr. & Mrs.	NEE
Mr. & Mrs.	NEE
Mr. & Mrs.	NEE
Mr. & Mrs.	NEE
Mr. & Mrs.	NEE
Mr. & Mrs.	NEE
Mr. & Mrs.	NEE
Mr. & Mrs.	NEE
Mr. & Mrs.	NEE
Mr. & Mrs.	NEE
Mr. & Mrs.	NEE
Mr. & Mrs.	NEE
Mr. & Mrs.	NEE
Mr. & Mrs.	NEE
Mr. & Mrs.	NEE
Mr. & Mrs.	NEE
Mr. & Mrs.	NEE
Mr. & Mrs.	NEE
Mr. & Mrs.	NEE
Mr. & Mrs.	NEE
Mr. & Mrs.	NEE
Mr. & Mrs.	NEE
Mr. & Mrs.	NEE
Mr. & Mrs.	NEE
Mr. & Mrs.	NEE
Mr. & Mrs.	NEE
Mr. & Mrs.	NEE
Mr. & Mrs.	NEE

The generations

preceding the one in the column on the left would have been born about 1800 and of course would be double the number.

Each generation going back in time will be twice the number. If your ancestors landed here in 1600 and you are under 30, you would be the 14th or 15th generation and be descended from over 16,000 people.

NEE REPRESENTS WIFE'S MAIDEN NAME

HUSBAND'S
ANCESTRAL CHART

Husband's Full Name

Date of Birth   Place of Birth

Date of Marriage   Place of Marriage

Date of Death   Place of Burial

Occupation

Special Interests

Grandfather's Full Name

Date of Birth   Place of Birth

Date of Marriage   Place of Marriage

Date of Death   Place of Burial

Occupation

Special Interests

Father's Full Name

Date of Birth   Place of Birth

Date of Marriage   Place of Marriage

Date of Death   Place of Burial

Occupation

Special Interests

Grandmother's Full Name

Date of Birth   Place of Birth

Date of Marriage   Place of Marriage

Date of Death   Place of Burial

Occupation

Special Interests

THE PRECEDING 3 GENERATIONS ON THE FOLLOWING PAGE

Grandfather's Full Name

Date of Birth   Place of Birth

Date of Marriage   Place of Marriage

Date of Death   Place of Burial

Occupation

Special Interests

Mother's Full Name

Date of Birth   Place of Birth

Date of Marriage   Place of Marriage

Date of Death   Place of Burial

Occupation

Special Interests

Grandmother's Full Name

Date of Birth   Place of Birth

Date of Marriage   Place of Marriage

Date of Death   Place of Burial

Occupation

Special Interests

Great Grandfather's Full Name

Date of Birth   Place of Birth

Occupation

Great Grandmother's Full Name

Date of Birth   Place of Birth

Special Interests

Great Grandfather's Full Name

Date of Birth   Place of Birth

Occupation

Great Grandmother's Full Name

Date of Birth   Place of Birth

Special Interests

Great Grandfather's Full Name

Date of Birth   Place of Birth

Occupation

Great Grandmother's Full Name

Date of Birth   Place of Birth

Special Interests

Great Grandfather's Full Name

Date of Birth   Place of Birth

Occupation

Great Grandmother's Full Name

Date of Birth   Place of Birth

Special Interests

Great, Great Grandfather's Full Name

Great, Great Grandmother's Full Name

Great, Great Grandfather's Full Name

Great, Great Grandmother's Full Name

Great, Great Grandfather's Full Name

Great, Great Grandmother's Full Name

Great, Great Grandfather's Full Name

Great, Great Grandmother's Full Name

Great, Great Grandfather's Full Name

Great, Great Grandmother's Full Name

Great, Great Grandfather's Full Name

Great, Great Grandmother's Full Name

Great, Great Grandfather's Full Name

Great, Great Grandmother's Full Name

Great, Great Grandfather's Full Name

Great, Great Grandmother's Full Name

Mr. & Mrs. _____ NEE _____

Mr. & Mrs. _____ NEE _____

Mr. & Mrs. _____ NEE _____

Mr. & Mrs. _____ NEE _____

Mr. & Mrs. _____ NEE _____

Mr. & Mrs. _____ NEE _____

Mr. & Mrs. _____ NEE _____

Mr. & Mrs. _____ NEE _____

Mr. & Mrs. _____ NEE _____

Mr. & Mrs. _____ NEE _____

Mr. & Mrs. _____ NEE _____

Mr. & Mrs. _____ NEE _____

Mr. & Mrs. _____ NEE _____

Mr. & Mrs. _____ NEE _____

Mr. & Mrs. _____ NEE _____

Mr. & Mrs. _____ NEE _____

Mr. & Mrs. _____ NEE _____

Mr. & Mrs. _____ NEE _____

Mr. & Mrs. _____ NEE _____

Mr. & Mrs. _____ NEE _____

Mr. & Mrs. _____ NEE _____

Mr. & Mrs. _____ NEE _____

Mr. & Mrs. _____ NEE _____

Mr. & Mrs. _____ NEE _____

Mr. & Mrs. _____ NEE _____

Mr. & Mrs. _____ NEE _____

Mr. & Mrs. _____ NEE _____

Mr. & Mrs. _____ NEE _____

Mr. & Mrs. _____ NEE _____

Mr. & Mrs. _____ NEE _____

Mr. & Mrs. _____ NEE _____

Mr. & Mrs. _____ NEE _____

For a variety of reasons, families have altered the spelling of the last name or changed it completely. So in looking back and trying to get information from the county, city or town overseas that your family came from, make sure you include as much data as you can before writing abroad.

NEE REPRESENTS WIFE'S MAIDEN NAME

HUSBAND'S FAMILY

On this and the next page, fill in all vital statistics on the husband, his brothers and sisters, and their children (nieces and nephews).

Husband, his Brothers and Sisters, and their Children	Born	Died	Spouse
Children			
Children			
Children			
Children			
Children			
Children			
Children			
Children			

Legal Guardians

Fill in the names of legal guardians for any child where applicable, including dates, places and any information you consider appropriate.

_____

_____

_____

_____

_____

_____

_____

_____

_____

_____

_____

_____

_____

_____

_____

_____

_____

_____

_____

_____

_____

HUSBAND'S
PARENTS' FAMILY

On this and the next page, fill in all vital statistics on the husband's parents, their brothers and sisters (aunts and uncles), and their children (cousins).

Husband's Father,
his Brothers and Sisters,
and their Children

	Born	Died	Spouse

Children

Children

Children

Children

Children

Children

Children

Children

Legal Guardians

Fill in the names of legal guardians for any child where applicable, including dates, places and any information you consider appropriate.

HUSBAND'S PARENTS' FAMILY

Continued

Husband's Mother,
her Brothers and Sisters,
and their Children

	Born	Died	Spouse

_____

Children —————————————————————

_____

Children —————————————————————

_____

Children —————————————————————

_____

Children —————————————————————

_____

Children —————————————————————

_____

Children —————————————————————

_____

Children —————————————————————

_____

Children —————————————————————

Legal Guardians

Fill in the names of legal guardians for any child where applicable, including dates, places and any information you consider appropriate.

HUSBAND'S GRANDPARENTS

FATHER'S SIDE

Grandfather, his Brothers and Sisters, and their Children	Born	Died	Spouse
Children			
Children			
Children			
Children			
Children			
Children			
Children			
Children			

Legal Guardians

Fill in the names of legal guardians for any child where applicable, including dates, places and any information you consider appropriate.

HUSBAND'S
GRANDPARENTS

Grandmother, her Brothers and Sisters, and their Children	Born	Died	Spouse
Children			
Children			
Children			
Children			
Children			
Children			
Children			
Children			

Legal Guardians

Fill in the names of legal guardians for any child where applicable, including dates, places and any information you consider appropriate.

HUSBAND'S
GRANDPARENTS

Grandfather, his Brothers and Sisters, and their Children	Born	Died	Spouse
Children			
Children			
Children			
Children			
Children			
Children			
Children			
Children			

Legal Guardians

Fill in the names of legal guardians for any child where applicable, including dates, places and any information you consider appropriate.

HUSBAND'S GRANDPARENTS

MOTHER'S SIDE

Continued

**Grandmother,
her Brothers and Sisters,
and their Children**

	Born	Died	Spouse

_____

Children _____

_____

Children _____

_____

Children _____

_____

Children _____

_____

Children _____

_____

Children _____

_____

Children _____

_____

Children _____

Legal Guardians

Fill in the names of legal guardians for any child where applicable, including dates, places and any information you consider appropriate.

HUSBAND'S GREAT GRANDPARENTS

Name	Born	Died	Spouse
Children			
Children			
Children			
Children			
Children			
Children			
Children			
Children			

Legal Guardians

Fill in the names of legal guardians for any child where applicable, including dates, places and any information you consider appropriate.

_____

_____

_____

_____

_____

_____

_____

_____

_____

_____

_____

_____

_____

_____

_____

_____

_____

_____

_____

_____

_____

WIFE'S
ANCESTRAL CHART

Wife's Full Name

Date of Birth   Place of Birth

Date of Marriage   Place of Marriage

Date of Death   Place of Burial

Occupation

Special Interests

Grandfather's Full Name
_____

Date of Birth   Place of Birth
_____

Date of Marriage   Place of Marriage
_____

Date of Death   Place of Burial
_____

Occupation
_____

Special Interests
_____

Father's Full Name
_____

Date of Birth   Place of Birth
_____

Date of Marriage   Place of Marriage
_____

Date of Death   Place of Burial
_____

Occupation
_____

Special Interests
_____

_____

Grandmother's Full Name
_____

Date of Birth   Place of Birth
_____

Date of Marriage   Place of Marriage
_____

Date of Death   Place of Burial
_____

Occupation
_____

Special Interests
_____

THE PRECEDING 3 GENERATIONS ON THE FOLLOWING PAGE

Grandfather's Full Name
_____

Date of Birth   Place of Birth
_____

Date of Marriage   Place of Marriage
_____

Date of Death   Place of Burial
_____

Occupation
_____

Special Interests
_____

Mother's Full Name
_____

Date of Birth   Place of Birth
_____

Date of Marriage   Place of Marriage
_____

Date of Death   Place of Burial
_____

Occupation
_____

Special Interests
_____

_____

Grandmother's Full Name
_____

Date of Birth   Place of Birth
_____

Date of Marriage   Place of Marriage
_____

Date of Death   Place of Burial
_____

Occupation
_____

Special Interests
_____

Great Grandfather's Full Name

Date of Birth   Place of Birth

Occupation

Great Grandmother's Full Name

Date of Birth   Place of Birth

Special Interests

Great Grandfather's Full Name

Date of Birth   Place of Birth

Occupation

Great Grandmother's Full Name

Date of Birth   Place of Birth

Special Interests

Great Grandfather's Full Name

Date of Birth   Place of Birth

Occupation

Great Grandmother's Full Name

Date of Birth   Place of Birth

Special Interests

Great Grandfather's Full Name

Date of Birth   Place of Birth

Occupation

Great Grandmother's Full Name

Date of Birth   Place of Birth

Special Interests

Great, Great Grandfather's Full Name

Great, Great Grandmother's Full Name

Great, Great Grandfather's Full Name

Great, Great Grandmother's Full Name

Great, Great Grandfather's Full Name

Great, Great Grandmother's Full Name

Great, Great Grandfather's Full Name

Great, Great Grandmother's Full Name

Great, Great Grandfather's Full Name

Great, Great Grandmother's Full Name

Great, Great Grandfather's Full Name

Great, Great Grandmother's Full Name

Great, Great Grandfather's Full Name

Great, Great Grandmother's Full Name

Great, Great Grandfather's Full Name

Great, Great Grandmother's Full Name

Great, Great, Great Grandparents

Mr. & Mrs.	NEE	
Mr. & Mrs.	NEE	
Mr. & Mrs.	NEE	
Mr. & Mrs.	NEE	
Mr. & Mrs.	NEE	
Mr. & Mrs.	NEE	
Mr. & Mrs.	NEE	
Mr. & Mrs.	NEE	
Mr. & Mrs.	NEE	
Mr. & Mrs.	NEE	
Mr. & Mrs.	NEE	
Mr. & Mrs.	NEE	
Mr. & Mrs.	NEE	
Mr. & Mrs.	NEE	
Mr. & Mrs.	NEE	
Mr. & Mrs.	NEE	
Mr. & Mrs.	NEE	
Mr. & Mrs.	NEE	
Mr. & Mrs.	NEE	
Mr. & Mrs.	NEE	
Mr. & Mrs.	NEE	
Mr. & Mrs.	NEE	
Mr. & Mrs.	NEE	
Mr. & Mrs.	NEE	
Mr. & Mrs.	NEE	
Mr. & Mrs.	NEE	
Mr. & Mrs.	NEE	
Mr. & Mrs.	NEE	
Mr. & Mrs.	NEE	
Mr. & Mrs.	NEE	
Mr. & Mrs.	NEE	
Mr. & Mrs.	NEE	

NEE REPRESENTS WIFE'S MAIDEN NAME

WIFE'S FAMILY

On this and the next page, fill in all vital statistics on the wife, her brothers and sisters, and their children (nieces and nephews).

Wife, her Brothers and Sisters, and their Children	Born	Died	Spouse
Children			
Children			
Children			
Children			
Children			
Children			
Children			
Children			

Legal Guardians

Fill in the names of legal guardians for any child where applicable, including dates, places and any information you consider appropriate.

WIFE'S PARENTS' FAMILY

On this and the next page, fill in all vital statistics on the wife's parents, their brothers and sisters (aunts and uncles), and their children (cousins).

**Wife's Father,
his Brothers and Sisters,
and their Children**

	Born	Died	Spouse
Children			
Children			
Children			
Children			
Children			
Children			
Children			
Children			

Legal Guardians

Fill in the names of legal guardians for any child where applicable, including dates, places and any information you consider appropriate.

WIFE'S PARENTS' FAMILY

Continued

Wife's Mother, her Brothers and Sisters, and their Children	Born	Died	Spouse
Children			
Children			
Children			
Children			
Children			
Children			
Children			
Children			

Legal Guardians

Fill in the names of legal guardians for any child where applicable, including dates, places and any information you consider appropriate.

WIFE'S GRANDPARENTS

FATHER'S SIDE

Grandfather, his Brothers and Sisters, and their Children	Born	Died	Spouse
Children			
Children			
Children			
Children			
Children			
Children			
Children			
Children			

Legal Guardians

Fill in the names of legal guardians for any child where applicable, including dates, places and any information you consider appropriate.

_____

_____

_____

_____

_____

_____

_____

_____

_____

_____

_____

_____

_____

_____

_____

_____

_____

_____

_____

_____

_____

_____

_____

_____

WIFE'S GRANDPARENTS

Grandmother, her Brothers and Sisters, and their Children	Born	Died	Spouse
Children			
Children			
Children			
Children			
Children			
Children			
Children			
Children			

Legal Guardians

Fill in the names of legal guardians for any child where applicable, including dates, places and any information you consider appropriate.

WIFE'S GRANDPARENTS

Grandfather,
his Brothers and Sisters,
and their Children   **Born**   **Died**   **Spouse**

_____   _____

Children ——————————————————————————————

_____   _____

Children ——————————————————————————————

_____   _____

Children ——————————————————————————————

_____   _____

Children ——————————————————————————————

_____   ————————————————————————————————

Children ——————————————————————————————

_____   ————————————————————————————————

Children ——————————————————————————————

_____   ————————————————————————————————

Children ——————————————————————————————

_____   ————————————————————————————————

Children ——————————————————————————————

Legal Guardians

Fill in the names of legal guardians for any child where applicable, including dates, places and any information you consider appropriate.

_____

_____

_____

_____

_____

_____

_____

_____

_____

_____

_____

_____

_____

_____

_____

_____

_____

_____

_____

_____

WIFE'S GRANDPARENTS

Grandmother, her Brothers and Sisters, and their Children	Born	Died	Spouse
Children			
Children			
Children			
Children			
Children			
Children			
Children			
Children			

Legal Guardians

Fill in the names of legal guardians for any child where applicable, including dates, places and any information you consider appropriate.

_____

_____

_____

_____

_____

_____

_____

_____

_____

_____

_____

_____

_____

_____

_____

_____

_____

_____

_____

_____

_____

_____

_____

_____

_____

WIFE'S GREAT GRANDPARENTS

Name	Born	Died	Spouse
Children			
Children			
Children			
Children			
Children			
Children			
Children			
Children			

Legal Guardians

Fill in the names of legal guardians for any child where applicable, including dates, places and any information you consider appropriate.

_____

_____

_____

_____

_____

_____

_____

_____

_____

_____

_____

_____

_____

_____

_____

_____

_____

_____

_____

_____

_____

_____

_____

_____

_____

CITIZENSHIP
RECORD

Name	Emigrated From	To	Date

Name	Emigrated From	To	Date

Name	Emigrated From	To	Date

In the space below fill in the countries your family came from along with any other information about that place you have or can get. Also put in when the family emigrated, where they landed and how your branch settled where it is now.

Name   Emigrated From   To   Date

_____   _____   _____   _____

_____

_____

_____

_____

Name   Emigrated From   To   Date

_____   _____   _____   _____

_____

_____

_____

_____

Name   Emigrated From   To   Date

_____   _____   _____   _____

_____

_____

_____

_____

Name   Emigrated From   To   Date

_____   _____   _____   _____

_____

_____

_____

_____

CITIZENSHIP RECORD

Continued

Name	Emigrated From	To	Date

Name	Emigrated From	To	Date

Name	Emigrated From	To	Date

EDDINGS

Names	Date	Place

Names	Date	Place

WEDDINGS

Continued

RELIGIOUS ACTIVITIES

Name	Ceremony or Occasion	Godparents or Sponsors	Date & Place

Name	Ceremony or Occasion	Godparents or Sponsors	Date & Place

RELIGIOUS ACTIVITIES

Continued

OUR PLACES OF WORSHIP

IN MEMORIAM

IN MEMORIAM

Continued

OUR HOMES

Street Address _____

City _____ State _____

Date of Purchase _____ Resided from _____ to _____

_____

_____

_____

_____

_____

_____

Street Address _____

City _____ State _____

Date of Purchase _____ Resided from _____ to _____

_____

_____

_____

_____

_____

_____

Street Address _____

City _____ State _____

Date of Purchase _____ Resided from _____ to _____

_____

_____

_____

_____

_____

_____

Street Address _____

City _____ State _____

Date of Purchase _____ Resided from _____ to _____

_____

_____

_____

_____

_____

_____

Street Address _____

City _____ State _____

Date of Purchase _____ Resided from _____ to _____

_____

_____

_____

_____

_____

Street Address _____

City _____ State _____

Date of Purchase _____ Resided from _____ to _____

_____

_____

_____

_____

_____

_____

Street Address _____

City _____ State _____

Date of Purchase _____ Resided from _____ to _____

_____

_____

_____

_____

_____

_____

Street Address _____

City _____ State _____

Date of Purchase _____ Resided from _____ to _____

_____

_____

_____

_____

_____

_____

WHERE OUR ANCESTORS HAVE LIVED

SCHOOLS
AND GRADUATIONS

Name	School, College or University	Dates of Attendance	Certificate or Degree

SCHOOLS
AND GRADUATIONS

Continued

IMPORTANT SCHOOL ACHIEVEMENTS — Fine Arts, Athletics, and Others

Name	Achievement	Date	School

CLUBS
AND ORGANIZATIONS

Name	Organization	Activity, Award, Office Held	Date

Fill in the names of family members and their clubs and organizations, including offices held and any other interesting information about the person or organization.

COMPANIES
WE HAVE WORKED
FOR OR OWNED

Record here employment histories and businesses started by any member of your family, including when and where a business was begun, and its success or failure and why.

COMPANIES
WE HAVE WORKED
FOR OR OWNED

Continued

SOCIAL SECURITY NUMBERS

MILITARY
SERVICE RECORDS

Name _____ Service Number _____ Job Classification _____

Enlisted or Inducted _____ Month _____ Day _____ Year _____ At Age _____

Branch of Service _____ Grade _____

Training Camps _____ Service Schools Attended _____

Division _____ Regiment _____ Department or Ship _____ Dates _____

Company _____ Transferred _____

Promotion and Dates _____

Overseas Service _____ Departure Date _____ Port _____ Return Date _____ Port _____

Battles, Engagements, Skirmishes, Expeditions _____ Commanding Officers _____ Citations _____

Wounds Received in Service; Sickness or Hospitalization _____

Important Leaves or Furloughs _____

Discharged at or Separation _____

Name _____ Service Number _____ Job Classification _____

Enlisted or Inducted _____ Month _____ Day _____ Year _____ At Age _____

Branch of Service _____ Grade _____

Training Camps _____ Service Schools Attended _____

_____

_____

_____

Division _____ Regiment _____ Department or Ship _____ Dates _____

Company _____ Transferred _____

Promotion and Dates _____

_____

_____

_____

Overseas Service _____ Departure Date _____ Port _____ Return Date _____ Port _____

_____

_____

_____

Battles, Engagements, Skirmishes, Expeditions _____ Commanding Officers _____ Citations _____

_____

_____

_____

_____

_____

Wounds Received in Service; Sickness or Hospitalization _____

_____

_____

_____

Important Leaves or Furloughs _____

Discharged at or Separation _____

MILITARY SERVICE RECORDS

Continued

Name _____ Service Number _____ Job Classification _____

Enlisted or Inducted _____ Month _____ Day _____ Year _____ At Age _____

Branch of Service _____ Grade _____

Training Camps _____ Service Schools Attended _____
_____

Division _____ Regiment _____ Department or Ship _____ Dates _____

Company _____ Transferred _____

Promotion and Dates _____
_____
_____

Overseas Service _____ Departure Date _____ Port _____ Return Date _____ Port _____
_____
_____

Battles, Engagements, Skirmishes, Expeditions _____ Commanding Officers _____ Citations _____
_____
_____

Wounds Received in Service; Sickness or Hospitalization _____
_____
_____

Important Leaves or Furloughs _____

Discharged at or Separation _____

Name _____ Service Number _____ Job Classification _____

Enlisted or Inducted _____ Month _____ Day _____ Year _____ At Age _____

Branch of Service _____ Grade _____

Training Camps _____ Service Schools Attended _____

_____

_____

Division _____ Regiment _____ Department or Ship _____ Dates _____

Company _____ Transferred _____

Promotion and Dates _____

_____

_____

Overseas Service _____ Departure Date _____ Port _____ Return Date _____ Port _____

_____

_____

_____

Battles, Engagements, Skirmishes, Expeditions _____ Commanding Officers _____ Citations _____

_____

_____

_____

Wounds Received in Service; Sickness or Hospitalization _____

_____

_____

_____

Important Leaves or Furloughs _____

Discharged at or Separation _____

MILITARY
SERVICE RECORDS

Continued

Name   Service Number   Job Classification

Enlisted or Inducted   Month   Day   Year   At Age

Branch of Service   Grade

Training Camps   Service Schools Attended

Division   Regiment   Department or Ship   Dates

Company   Transferred

Promotion and Dates

Overseas Service   Departure Date   Port   Return Date   Port

Battles, Engagements, Skirmishes, Expeditions   Commanding Officers   Citations

Wounds Received in Service; Sickness or Hospitalization

Important Leaves or Furloughs

Discharged at or Separation

Name   Service Number   Job Classification

Enlisted or Inducted   Month   Day   Year   At Age

Branch of Service   Grade

Training Camps   Service Schools Attended

Division   Regiment   Department or Ship   Dates

Company   Transferred

Promotion and Dates

Overseas Service   Departure Date   Port   Return Date   Port

Battles, Engagements, Skirmishes, Expeditions   Commanding Officers   Citations

Wounds Received in Service; Sickness or Hospitalization

Important Leaves or Furloughs

Discharged at or Separation

MILITARY SERVICE RECORDS

Continued

Name _____ Service Number _____ Job Classification _____

Enlisted or Inducted _____ Month _____ Day _____ Year _____ At Age _____

Branch of Service _____ Grade _____

Training Camps _____ Service Schools Attended _____

_____

Division _____ Regiment _____ Department or Ship _____ Dates _____

Company _____ Transferred _____

Promotion and Dates _____

_____

_____

Overseas Service _____ Departure Date _____ Port _____ Return Date _____ Port _____

_____

_____

Battles, Engagements, Skirmishes, Expeditions _____ Commanding Officers _____ Citations _____

_____

_____

Wounds Received in Service; Sickness or Hospitalization _____

_____

_____

Important Leaves or Furloughs _____

Discharged at or Separation _____

Name   Service Number   Job Classification

Enlisted or Inducted   Month   Day   Year   At Age

Branch of Service   Grade

Training Camps   Service Schools Attended

Division   Regiment   Department or Ship   Dates

Company   Transferred

Promotion and Dates

Overseas Service   Departure Date   Port   Return Date   Port

Battles, Engagements, Skirmishes, Expeditions   Commanding Officers   Citations

Wounds Received in Service; Sickness or Hospitalization

Important Leaves or Furloughs

Discharged at or Separation

SPECIAL FRIENDS

Everyone has a special friend who sometimes seems like part of the family. Certainly they make up some big parts of your life, so including them in a family record book seems appropriate. Don't forget to include dates, addresses and some of those things that make these people so special.

_____

_____

_____

_____

_____

_____

_____

_____

_____

_____

_____

_____

_____

FAMILY PETS

_____

_____

_____

_____

_____

Owner	Pet's Name	Type of Pet	Dates of Ownership
_____	_____	_____	_____
_____	_____	_____	_____
_____	_____	_____	_____
_____	_____	_____	_____
_____	_____	_____	_____
_____	_____	_____	_____
_____	_____	_____	_____
_____	_____	_____	_____

The chances are millions to one that you have a pet elephant but more likely you have a dog, cat, turtle or fish. Animals, like good friends, seem to become part of the family and play a part in our daily lives. Because they are integrated into the 'family,' remembering them will recall fond memories.

FAMILY AUTOMOBILES

Owner	Make, Model, Year	Color	Dates of Ownership

Americans have always been a people on the move and ever since Henry ford started to mass produce cars they have been a part of almost every family's life. Every auto you have owned or will own has a special place in your life and remembering them will bring back lots of memories.

FAVORITE THINGS

HIS AND HERS

Songs, Records, Books,
Shows, Places, Recipes, etc.

_____

_____

_____

_____

_____

_____

_____

_____

_____

_____

_____

_____

_____

_____

_____

_____

_____

_____

_____

_____

CHILDREN

Songs, Records, Stories, Toys,
Places, Pastimes, etc.

COLLECTIONS
AND HEIRLOOMS

Include here special collections of various family members—what they are, when begun, how much collected, etc. List all heirlooms, including original owner and how items were passed from generation to generation. In short, record anything of interest to you that will also be of interest to others who read about your family.

COLLECTIONS
AND HEIRLOOMS

Continued

FAVORITE FAMILY SPORTS

Family or Individual's Name	Sport, Team, Club	Special Achievement

Family or Individual's Name	Sport, Team, Club	Special Achievement

FAVORITE FAMILY SPORTS

Continued

FAVORITE FAMILY HOBBIES

_____

_____

_____

_____

_____

_____

_____

_____

_____

_____

_____

_____

_____

_____

_____

_____

_____

_____

_____

From woodcarving and quiltmaking to rebuilding old cars and raising exotic plants, many families have individuals who pursue a wide variety of interesting hobbies. Here is a space to record those individuals and their pastimes and any fascinating pieces of information about how they started and why, and whether anyone else followed in their footsteps.

FAVORITE FAMILY HOBBIES

Continued

FAMILY VACATIONS

Getting away from it all seems to keep us going through the rest of the year so entering some of the places you go to, who was there, and what happened can help bring back some of that fun. Some vacations are not so much where you went as what you did or who you met, so by recording this you have the chance, in the future, to look back and smile or cry.

_____

_____

_____

_____

_____

_____

_____

_____

_____

_____

_____

_____

FAMILY REUNIONS

Remembering

who was there and at what occasion is a lot easier if you record it here. In years to come this kind of information will conjure up the event all over again for you— no matter if it was your fifth high school class reunion or your Fiftieth Wedding Anniversary.

FAMILY REUNIONS

Continued

FAMILY TRADITIONS

EVENTS
TO REMEMBER

Here you may record information about events (other than such things as reunions, trips and club activities) that you may want to recall years from now. Include family "firsts" and unique achievements—winning a special prize, meeting a famed personality, witnessing an outstanding event.

EVENTS
TO REMEMBER

Continued

ORAL FAMILY HISTORY

From survivors and participants in wars to migrations from other countries, each family has stories no one has ever written down. Here is a space to do so to record forever what would be lost if it remains "oral history."

_____

_____

_____

_____

_____

_____

_____

_____

_____

_____

_____

_____

_____

ORAL FAMILY HISTORY

Continued

EXTRAORDINARY EVENTS

WE HAVE SURVIVED AND OVERCOME

Into each family comes those unforeseen events. Many have survived natural disasters (floods, tornados) and many times families were forced to move or were altered for the better as a result. Here is a space for you to record whatever you feel is appropriate in relation to your own family's experiences.

ILLNESSES

Name	Illness, Operation	Hospital, Doctor	Date

VITAL STATISTICS

Space is provided on these pages for vital statistics.
Fill in with as much detail as you care to note.

HIS

Height _____

Weight _____

Hair Color _____

Eye Color _____

Suit Size _____

Shirt Size _____

Waist _____

Shoe Size _____

Hat Size _____

Ring Size _____

Other Sizes _____

_____

_____

Color Preference _____

_____

_____

Toiletries Preferences _____

_____

_____

HERS

Height _____

Weight _____

Hair Color _____

Eye Color _____

Blouse Size _____

Dress Size _____

Shoe Size _____

Ring Size _____

Other Sizes _____

_____

_____

_____

_____

_____

_____

Color Preference _____

_____

_____

_____

_____

_____

Perfume and Toiletries Preferences _____

_____

_____

_____

_____

VITAL STATISTICS

Continued

CHILDREN	Height	Weight	Hair Color	Eye Color

Color Preference _____

CHILDREN

Suit Size	Shirt Size	Shoe Size	Hat Size	Ring Size	Other Size

PHOTOGRAPHS

Pictures do their own story telling and in years to come a lot can be learned from this kind of record. You and future generations will be able to look back and see a member of the family in his or her own time and place. (You may also want to include favorite clippings, mementos, or documents.)

PHOTOGRAPHS

PHOTOGRAPHS

GENEALOGY
RESEARCH

All of us know something about our living relatives. We enjoy telling stories about their achievements and exploits, and we certainly have a fondness for the endearing characters that are in most families. Yet our knowledge of our families often does not go beyond those members we actually know. Few of us have been lucky enough to have known our great-grandparents for example. This shows us that one of the most common ways of learning about ourselves is by word of mouth; the so-called oral tradition. Thus, if you want to begin finding out more about your family the place to start is with your relatives. Ask them if they can provide you with birth dates, places of residence and dates of death of those whom you do not know, such as your great-grandparents. Do this as far as it is possible to trace them. Also, check to see if there are any relatives who have previous-

OUR FAMILY TREE

ly done genealogical research that might aid in your search. Once you have reached this point you will discover the great treasures of information available in family bibles, picture, albums, old letters, diaries and account books. Your ancestors often kept better records than you think!

If you have access to a computer, search the Internet for surnames you have found (mother's maiden name, grandmother's maiden name, etc.) You might discover some useful information or even come across others who are doing research on the same lines of genealogy as you. There are many websites and message boards

devoted entirely to genealogy. Check them out, look for surnames, get what help you can from them.

Once you have names, dates and places you can consult town records. Securing birth certificates, marriage licenses, death certificates, wills and land deeds will give you additional names you will want and need. Don't be disappointed if some of these public records are not available. You can always check your public library. Some of the subjects you can look up at the library are clans, deeds, epitaphs, estates, marriage licenses, nobility, parish registers, peerage and precedence. Also don't forget to ask the librarian for additional sources of genealogical information. If the books listed in the card catalogue are not in the stacks, your librarian can easily send for them.

Another place to check is your state genealogical association or historical society. Each state has its own organization with qualified people who can be very helpful in local matters. These associations also often publish their own periodicals that you might like to look into. The Daughters of the American Revolution in your area may also be able to furnish you with further information. Sometimes they too publish interesting pamphlets on the subject.

The next step in your search is to contact the National Archives, which is the central United States depository for records, located in Washington, D.C., to find out which of their eleven regional branches is nearest you. The National Archives contain many different kinds of records which will be helpful to you. The Census Records, from 1790 to date, are kept here. They give information such as the name of each family member, age, occupation and place of birth. Also available are records of military service, pensions and land grants. Since we are a nation of immigrants you may find here the names of the first members of your family who came to America, as well as the name of the ship that brought them, the date of arrival, the port of entry and the date of naturalization. For other such information one should consult the United States Immigration and Naturalization office.

For the majority of us our families have only lived in America for three or four generations. It was about this time that the mass immigrations from other countries to the United States began. Thus far, all of the research information has concentrated on relatives who lived in America. There is no need to stop researching at this point however, because there are sources available to help you trace your ancestors to the countries that they originally came from. The library of the Church of Jesus Christ of Latter-Day Saints in Salt Lake City contains the largest collection of genealogical information dating from 1538 to 1805. It contains records from the national and local archives, courthouses, cemeteries, churches and a variety of other places where records were kept, about people all over the world. Some 40 countries are represented in this collection of genealogical data. This enormous library has branches around the world and since they require that you do your own research you can contact them to find out which of the twenty branches is closest to you. The library's researchers are continually making copies of genealogical records throughout the world to further expand the collection.

For the most part, at this point your have completed all of the research that can be done in America and it is time to write away to foreign countries to get additional information. To find out where and to whom to write you should contact the consulate of the country to which you are writing. Once the consulate has sent you the correct address and the name of the person to whom you should write, do not hesitate because you don't speak the language; the agency will get someone to translate your letter for them. It is very important to include as much pertinent information as you have. Names, dates, places of residence are especially necessary. One thing you must consider is that often when people arrived in America from other countries their names were misspelled or arbitrarily anglicized and therefore you must know what their name was originally before you make any inquiries.

Do not get discouraged, as you can see there are many sources to help you find information. To give you an idea of what results your search for your roots can lead to, let us take an historical example. It has been over 350 years since the arrival of the Mayflower in 1620, which means there have been about 13 generations of your family since that time. These 13 generations represent more than 16,000 direct descendants.

To account for all of these ancestors in order to have a complete genealogical chart would be an imposing task even for an expert and, if you continued to expand the charts used in this book, by the time you reached 1600 that column would have over 8,000 spaces for names and be over 165 feet tall. If you decide after doing some searching on your own that you need the help of a professional researcher, research and contact qualified genealogists. Some people who did not have a written language will have to rely on the records of others. To say the least, at most times they are inaccurate and distorted. Even the South American Indians, who did have a written language, lost it, so all natives of the Western Hemisphere and Black Africans will have to seek out oral family or tribal histories which many times cannot pinpoint a place, person, or date but in general are quite close to fact. Do not be taken in by the commercially advertised mail-order coat-of-arms trade.

The charts that appear in this book go back five generations, about 150 years. These five generations represent about 124 people in a direct line descendancy.

ADDRESSES TO WRITE TO:

Where to write for booklets on how and where to find vital records:

Superintendent of Documents
United States Government Printing Office
732 N. Capital St., NW
Washington, D.C. 20402
Ph: 1-888-293-6498
http://bookstore.gpo.gov
"Where to Write for Vital Records:
Births, Deaths, and Divorces" 2003
(Public Health Service Publication, $4.25)

The Church of Jesus Christ of Latter-Day Saints
50 E. North Temple Street
Salt Lake City, Utah 84150
Ph: 1-801-240-1000
www.familysearch.org

The National Archives and Records Administration
8601 Adelphi Road

College Park, MD 20740-6001
Ph: 1-866-272-6272
www.archives.gov

Board for the Certification of Genealogists
P.O Box 14291
Washington, D.C. 20044
www.bcgcertification.org

BOOKSTORES WHICH SPECIALIZE IN GENEALOGICAL MATERIAL

Genealogical Publishing Co., Inc.
1001 N. Calvert Street
Baltimore, MD 21202-3897
Ph: 1-800-296-6687
Fax: 1-410-752-8492
Orders: sales@genealogical.com
www.genealogical.com

Higginson Book Company
148 Washington Street
Salem, MA 01970
Ph: 1-978-745-7170
Fax: 1-978-745-8025
Orders: orders@higginsonbooks.com
www.higginsonbooks.com

Tuttle Antiquarian Books Inc.
28 South Main Street
Rutland, VT 05701
Ph: 1-802-773-8229
Fax: 1-802-773-1493
Contact: tuttbook@sover.net
www.tuttlebooks.com

Willow Bend Books Bookstore
Customer Service Division
65 E. Main Street
Westminster, MD 21157
Ph: 1-800-876-6103
Fax: 1-410-871-2674
Contact: info@heritagebooks.com
www.heritagebooks.com

PUBLICATIONS:

Family Chronicle Magazine
(www.familychronicle.com)

Family Tree Magazine
(www.familytreemagazine.com)

Everton's Family History Magazine
(www.everton.com)

Eastman's Online Genealogy Newsletter
(www.eogn.com)

Heritage Quest
(www.heritagequest.com)

Journal of Online Genealogy
(www.onlinegenealogy.com)

Ancestor News
(www.ancestornews.com)

HELPFUL WEBSITES

www.cyndislist.com (Guide, information, websites, tips)
www.ancestry.com (Genealogy)
www.rootsweb.com (Genealogy)
www.onegreatfamily.com (Genealogy)
www.genealogytoday.com (Genealogy)
www.genealogytoday.com/ca (Genealogy, Canadian)
www.ellisisland.org (Ellis Island)
www.usgenweb.org (USGenWeb Project)

www.rootsweb.com/~canwgw/ (Canada GenWeb Project)
www.loc.gov/rr/genealogy (Library of Congress)
www.ingeneas.com (Genealogy, Canadian)
www.acgs.org (American-Canadian Genealogical Society)
www.collectionscanada.ca (Library and Archives Canada)
www.allvitalrecords.com (Birth, census, marriage, death records)
http://newspaperarchive.com (Searchable newspapers dating back to 1748)

BIBLIOGRAPHY

American Genealogical Research Institute. **How to Trace Your Family Tree.** Dolphin Books.
Bennett, Archibald F. **Finding Your Forefathers in America.** Salt Lake City, Bookcraft Co., 1957.
Bidlack, Russell Eugene. **First Steps in Climbing the Family Tree.** Detroit Society for Genealogical Research, 1966.
Doane, Gilbert H. **Searching for Your Ancestors.** New York, Bantam Books, Inc., 1974.
Everton, George B. **The Handybook for Genealogist.** Logan, Utah, Everton Publishers, 1962.

Greenwood, Val D. **The Researcher's Guide to American Genealogy.** Genealogical Publishing Co., 1973.
Iredale, David. **Discovering Your Family Tree.** Shire Publications.
National Genealogical Society. Special Publications: No. 17, **Genealogy, Handmaid of History.**
(A list can be obtained of other articles on the subject from the Society, 1921 Sunderland Place, N.W., Washington, D.C. 20036)
Rottenberg, Dan. **Finding Our Fathers.** New York, Random House, 1977.
Williams, Ethel W. **Know Your Ancestors.** Rutland, Vt., C.E. Tuttle Co., 1964.